D1716408

HYENAS
ON THE HUNT

by Jody Sullivan Rake

Reading Consultant:
Barbara J. Fox
Reading Specialist
North Carolina State University

Content Consultant:
Kay E. Holekamp, PhD
Department of Zoology
Michigan State University
East Lansing, Michigan

CAPSTONE PRESS
a capstone imprint

Blazers is published by Capstone Press,
151 Good Counsel Drive, P.O. Box 669, Mankato, Minnesota 56002.
www.capstonepress.com

092009
005619WZS10

 Books published by Capstone Press are manufactured with paper
containing at least 10 percent post-consumer waste.

Library of Congress Cataloging-in-Publication Data
Rake, Jody Sullivan.
    Hyenas : on the hunt / by Jody Sullivan Rake.
    p. cm. — (Blazers. Killer animals)
    Summary: "Describes Hyenas, their habitat, hunting habits, and relationship to
people" — Provided by publisher.
    Includes bibliographical references and index.
    ISBN 978-1-4296-3926-2 (library binding)
    1. Hyenas — Juvenile literature. I. Title.
QL737.C24R35 2010
599.74'3 — dc22   2009027859

Editorial Credits
Mandy Robbins, editor; Kyle Grenz, designer; Svetlana Zhurkin, media researcher;
    Laura Manthe, production specialist

Photo Credits
Brand X Pictures, 26–27
Corbis/Yann Arthus-Bertrand, 22–23, 28–29
Creatas, 18–19
Minden Pictures/Andrew Parkinson, 20–21; Mitsuaki Iwago, 4–5, 6–7; Suzi Eszterhas, 16–17
Nature Picture Library/Anup Shah, cover
Peter Arnold/Biosphere/Dennis Nigel, 12–13; Gunther Michel, 24–25
Photolibrary/Uwe Skrzypczak, 10–11
Shutterstock/Antonio Jorge Nunes, 8–9; Gail Johnson, 14–15

TABLE OF CONTENTS

AGGRESSIVE HUNTERS

Under the hot African sun, a deadly race is on. Hyenas are chasing a **wildebeest** across the **savanna**.

wildebeest – a large African animal with a head like an ox, two curved horns, and a long tail

savanna – a flat, grassy area of land with few or no trees

The hyenas pounce on the wildebeest. There is a loud thud, and the hyenas crowd around their prize. Their strong jaws rip into the wildebeest.

KILLER FACT

Hyenas live mainly in the grasslands of eastern and southern Africa.

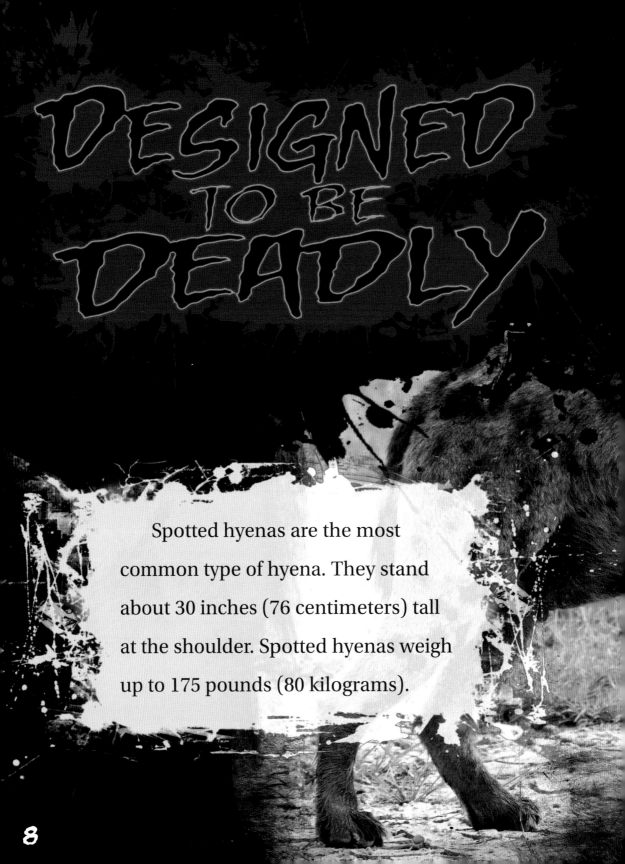

DESIGNED TO BE DEADLY

Spotted hyenas are the most common type of hyena. They stand about 30 inches (76 centimeters) tall at the shoulder. Spotted hyenas weigh up to 175 pounds (80 kilograms).

KILLER FACT

There are four types of hyenas.
They are the spotted, striped, and brown
hyenas, and the aardwolf.

The hyena's most amazing weapons are its teeth and jaws. Its sharp **canine teeth** pierce **prey's** skin and muscle. The hyena's strong jaws crush bones.

canine teeth – sharp teeth used to tear meat

prey – an animal that is hunted by another animal

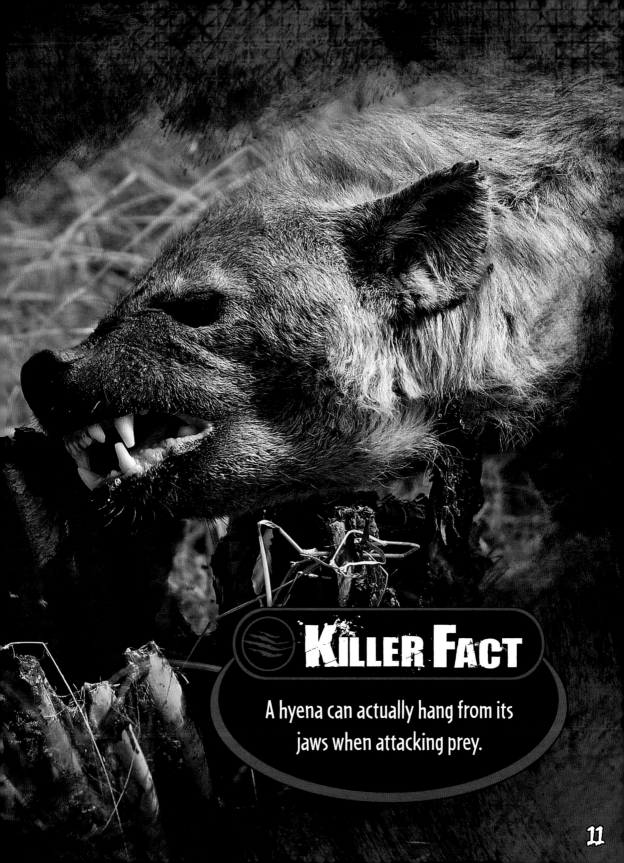

KILLER FACT

A hyena can actually hang from its jaws when attacking prey.

KILLER FACT

Hyenas can travel 19 miles
(31 kilometers) in one day.

Long front legs and muscular shoulders help hyenas run long distances. They sprint up to 30 miles (48 kilometers) per hour. Hyenas can run for hours without stopping.

Hyena Diagram

muscular
shoulders

strong jaws

long front legs

ECO-FRIENDLY HUNTER

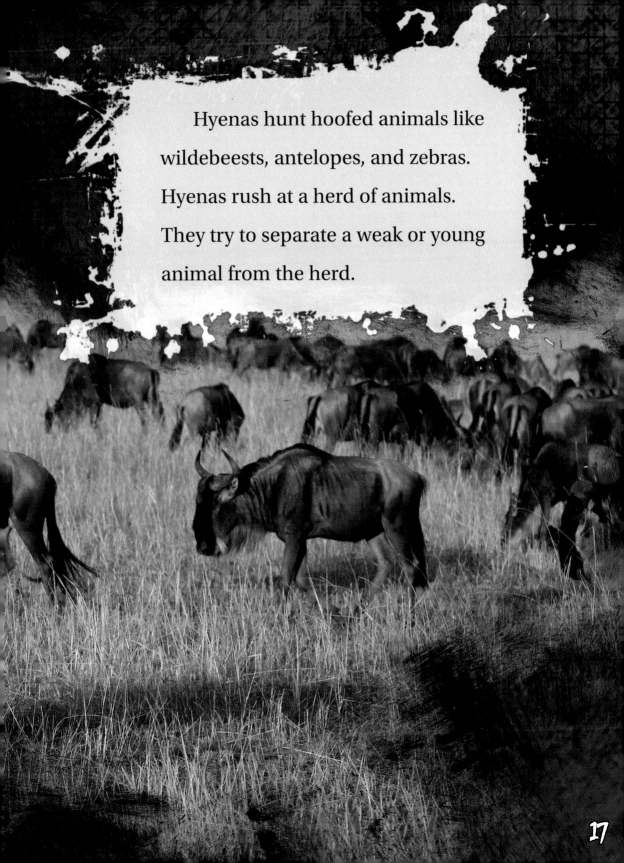

Hyenas hunt hoofed animals like wildebeests, antelopes, and zebras. Hyenas rush at a herd of animals. They try to separate a weak or young animal from the herd.

Hyenas are also **scavengers**. They eat dead animals left by other **predators**. Scavengers clear the land of dead, rotting flesh.

scavenger – an animal that feeds on animals that are already dead

predator – an animal that hunts other animals for food

KILLER FACT

Hyenas even eat the skin and bones of prey. Only horns and hooves are left behind.

Hyenas are important for a healthy **ecosystem**. As hunters, they take out the weak members of a herd. As scavengers, they rid the land of dead animals.

ecosystem – a group of animals and plants that work together with their surroundings

NO LAUGHING MATTER

Hyenas have no real predators. But they do compete with lions for food. Lions chase and sometimes attack hyenas.

KILLER FACT

Spotted hyenas may make a laughing
sound when they are frightened.

Hyenas can be dangerous to people. But they usually won't attack people unless prey is hard to find.

KILLER FACT

Some African tribes do not bury their dead.
Instead, they leave the bodies outside
for hyenas to eat.

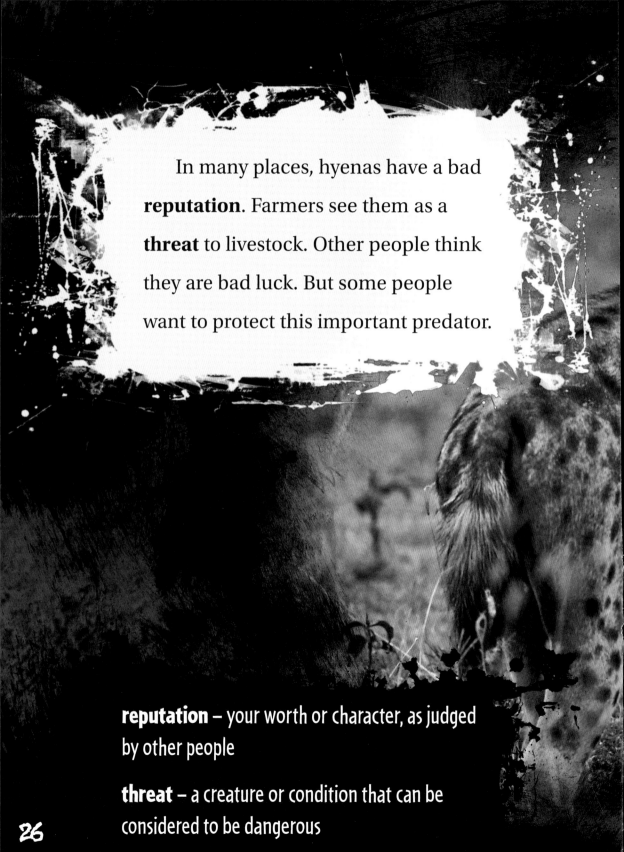

In many places, hyenas have a bad **reputation**. Farmers see them as a **threat** to livestock. Other people think they are bad luck. But some people want to protect this important predator.

reputation – your worth or character, as judged by other people

threat – a creature or condition that can be considered to be dangerous

Attack!

GLOSSARY

canine teeth (KAY-nyn TEETH) — sharp teeth used to tear meat

ecosystem (EE-koh-sis-tuhm) — a group of animals and plants that work together with their surroundings

predator (PRED-uh-tur) — an animal that hunts other animals for food

prey (PRAY) — an animal that is hunted by another animal as food

reputation (rep-yuh-TAY-shuhn) — your worth or character, as judged by other people

savanna (suh-VAN-uh) — a flat, grassy area of land with few or no trees

scavenger (SKAV-uhn-jer) — an animal that feeds on animals that are already dead

threat (THRET) — a creature or condition that can be considered to be dangerous

wildebeest (WIL-duh-beest) — a large African animal with a head like an ox, two curved horns, and a long tail

READ MORE

Malam, John. *Hyenas.* Scary Creatures. New York: Franklin Watts, 2008.

Markle, Sandra. *Hyenas.* Animal Scavengers. Minneapolis: Lerner, 2005.

Pearl, Norman. *Hyenas: Fierce Hunters.* Powerful Predators. New York: Rosen, 2009.

INTERNET SITES

FactHound offers a safe, fun way to find Internet sites related to this book. All of the sites on FactHound have been researched by our staff.

Here's all you do:

Visit *www.facthound.com*

FactHound will fetch the best sites for you!

INDEX